AF267438

NATIVE AMERICAN HERBALISM BIBLE 3

By

ROSEMARY KENNEDY

© Copyright 2021 by Rosemary Kennedy.
All rights reserved.

This document is geared towards providing exact and reliable information regarding the topic and issue covered. The publication is sold with the idea that the publisher is not required to render accounting, officially permitted or otherwise qualified services. If advice is necessary, legal or professional, a practiced individual in the profession should be ordered.

From a Declaration of Principles, this was accepted and approved equally by a Committee of the American Bar Association and a Committee of Publishers and Associations.

In no way is it legal to reproduce, duplicate, or transmit any part of this document in either electronic means or printed format. Recording of this publication is strictly prohibited, and any storage of this document is not allowed unless with written permission from the publisher. All rights reserved.

The information provided herein is stated to be truthful and consistent, in that any liability, in terms of inattention or otherwise, by any usage or abuse of any policies, processes, or Instructions contained within is the solitary and utter responsibility of the recipient reader. Under no circumstances will any legal responsibility or blame be held against the publisher for reparation, damages, or monetary loss due to the information herein, either directly or indirectly.

Respective authors own all copyrights not held by the publisher.

The information herein is offered for informational purposes solely and is universal as such. The presentation of the information is without a contract or any type of guarantee assurance.

The trademarks used are without any consent, and the publication of the trademark is without permission or backing by the trademark owner. All trademarks and brands within this book are for clarifying purposes only and are owned by the owners themselves, not affiliated with this document.

Table of Contents

INTRODUCTION

In ancient times, man uses natural medicines to fight against viral and bacterial diseases. The methods of utilizing the natural resources were preserved through different methods and were transferred from generation to generation to benefit from their ancestor's knowledge. But with the advancement in the science and technology world, the focus is shifted from natural cure to synthetic cure. The modern man has gone far away from the natural resources, and the ancestors' knowledge has gone back the shelf. But the synthetic world and its treatment options have come with many drawbacks. Thus, now the scientists and researchers have again opened up the books of their forefathers to find the solution based on natural resources.

When we talk or read about herbalism, Native Americans of North America are among the early users of herbs. Native Americans find herbs as a vital part of their daily life to fight against various diseases. But the people of the modern world are business-minded. They take everything for their business and progress, even if it's the health of the common people. They take advantage of that too; that is why they have taken the people away from the cost-effective and radially available solution to the complex diseases they encounter.

With the increase in disease and people affected, research was conducted to compare the Modern Age and the Stone Age. And interestingly, researchers have found out that people who were living thousands of years ago or at least when this modern medicine has not popular and advanced as today, were healthier than the modern man. They have good health with fewer diseases even though their resources were very limited compared with modern man.

The reason for being healthier than us is that older people knew that the well-being of man is solely dependent on peace of their mind, soul and body. If their minds, souls, and bodies work in harmony and are in peace, their overall health will be more than good. But if any of these three are not working properly, then the body will suffer in the form of diseases or infection. Thus, our forefathers always keep a balance between these three factors of life. At their times, the man was very close to nature because of their limited resources, and this closeness benefitted them a lot. This has encountered many natural resources that helped them balance their soul, mind, and body. In this regard, the Native Americans have collected data of more than 500 various herbs extracted from the Earth and organized them along with their preparation and use at one place so that their coming generations will also benefit from their discovery. Ancient Native Americans have played their part by discovering, gathering and organizing the knowledge in one place and handed it over to us. It is our responsibility to gain the advantage of their knowledge and further explore this area of nature.

This book will give you a platform to get to know about the traditions of the Native Americans about using herbal medicines. You may get guidance on how nature will help you to bring the three elements of your life, brain, soul and body, in harmony. You will learn about using nature as an alternative to modern medicines, to cut down your medical cost and other such expenses. Thus, Native American herbal remedies provide you with a huge platform to explore nature in its true form. Hence, this book is a source of knowledge of healing yourself with nature and developing and strengthening your connections with nature, to get more and more benefits from it even more than original Native Americans.

CHAPTER 1:
MOST COMMON DIY RECIPES

TEAS

1. COLD CARE TEA

Ingredients:

- ¼ tsp. sage leaves.
- ¼ tsp. calendula flower.
- ¼ tsp. elderflower.
- ¼ tsp. hibiscus flower.

Instructions:

1. Boil the water in a pot.
2. Add all the ingredients to the serving cup and mix well.
3. Pour boiling water into the serving cup with the mixture.
4. Cover the cup and steep it for 8 minutes.
5. You can mix in honey as per your taste.
6. Serve and enjoy it.

2. RESPIRATORY SUPPORT TEA

Ingredients:

- ¼ tsp. marshmallow root.
- 1/3 tsp. mullein.
- ¼ tsp. rose hips.
- ¼ tsp. lemon balm.
- ¼ tsp. osha root.
- ¼ tsp. coltsfoot leaves.

Instructions:

1. Boil the water in a pot.
2. Mix Osha and marshmallow roots.
3. Cover the pot and let it cook for 10 minutes at a low flame.
4. Stir in the remaining items and mix well.
5. Cover the pot again and let it steep for 10 minutes.
6. You can mix in honey as per your taste.
7. Strain the tea in serving cups.
8. Serve and enjoy it.

3. CAYENNE TEA

Ingredients:

- 1/8 tsp. cayenne powder.
- 1 tsp. honey.
- 2 tsp. lemon juice.

Instructions:

1. Boil the water in a pot.
2. Add all the ingredients to the serving cup and mix well.
3. Pour boiling water into a serving cup with lemon mixture.
4. Cover the cup and steep it for 8 minutes.
5. You can mix in honey as per your taste.
6. Serve and enjoy it.

4. EASY MASALA TEA

Ingredients:

- 1 tsp. cinnamon.
- 1 tsp. ginger.
- 1 tsp. cardamom.
- ½ clove.
- 1 tsp. black tea leaves.
- ¼ tsp. black peppercorns.
- 2 c water.
- 1 ½ c milk.

Instructions:

1. First, crush cinnamon, peppercorn, cardamom, and cloves in a mortar system.
2. Add water to a pan and bring it to a boil.
3. Add the crushed spices and ginger.
4. Reduce the flame to low and cover the pan.
5. Let it simmer for 20 minutes.
6. Stir in milk and tea leaves.
7. Cover the pan again and cook it for 7 minutes.

8. Remove the pan from the flame and let it steep for six more minutes.

9. You can add honey or sugar as per your taste.

10. Strain the tea in serving cups.

11. Serve and enjoy it.

5. HERBAL TEA

Ingredients:

- 1/3 tsp. elderberries.

- 1/3 tsp. rose hips.

- 1/3 tsp. Echinacea.

- 1/3 tsp. chamomile.

- 1/3 tsp. astragals.

Instructions:

1. Boil the water in a pot.
2. Add all the ingredients to the serving cup and mix well.
3. Pour boiling water into the serving cup with the mixture.
4. Cover the cup and steep it for 8 minutes.
5. You can mix in honey as per your taste.
6. Serve and enjoy it.

6. CALMING MARSHMALLOW ROSE TEA

Ingredients:

- 1 tsp. marshmallow root.

- 1 tsp. rosebuds.

- 1 tsp. cassia cinnamon chips.

- 1 tsp. Tulsi leaves (holy basil).

Instructions:

1. Boil the water in a pot.
2. Add all the ingredients to the serving cup and mix well.
3. Pour boiling water into the serving cup with the mixture.
4. Cover the cup and steep it for 8 minutes.
5. You can mix in honey as per your taste.
6. Strain the tea.
7. Serve and enjoy it.

7. LAVENDER TEA

Ingredients:

- 2 c water.

- 5 tbsp. lemon balm.

- 2 tbsp. lavender flower, dried.

- 1 tbsp. honey.

Instructions:

1. Boil the water in a pot.
2. Add all the ingredients to the serving cup and mix well.
3. Pour boiling water into a serving cup with lemon balm mixture.
4. Cover the cup and steep it for 8 minutes.
5. You can mix in honey as per your taste.
6. Strain the tea.
7. Serve and enjoy it.

8. AUTUMN TONIC TEA

Ingredients:

- 2 tsp. nettle leaves.
- 1 1/3 tsp. lemon balm.
- 2 c water.
- 1 1/3 tsp. of spearmint.
- 1 tsp. mullein.
- 1 tsp. ginger.
- 1 ½ tsp. dandelion.
- 1 tsp. rose hips.
- 1 tsp. red clover.

Instructions:

1. Boil the water in a pot.
2. Add all the ingredients to the serving cup and mix well.
3. Pour boiling water into the serving cup with the mixture.
4. Cover the cup and steep it for 15 minutes.
5. You can mix in honey as per your taste.
6. Serve and enjoy it.

9. BLACK APPLE TEA MIX

Ingredients:

- 1/3 c chopped sweet apple.
- 1/3 tsp. lemon juice.
- 1 clove.
- ¼ tsp. cinnamon.
- ½ tsp. honey.
- 1 tsp. black tea leaves.

Instructions:

1. Add apple and lemon juice to a bowl.
2. Pour in water and keep it aside for 10 minutes.
3. Bake the apple slices in preheated oven at 300 F° for 85 minutes.
4. After baking, crush the apples and mix in all the remaining items.
5. You can store this mixture in an airtight container.
6. When in need of black apple tea, boil the water in a pot.
7. Add 1 tbsp. apple mixture to the serving cup and mix well.
8. Pour boiling water into the serving cup with the mixture.

9. Cover the cup and steep it for 8 minutes.

10. You can mix in honey as per your taste.

11. Serve and enjoy it.

10. DIGESTIVE TEA

Ingredients:

- 1 tbsp. spearmint.

- ¼ tsp. of licorice root, dried.

Instructions:

1. Boil the water in a pot.
2. Add all the ingredients to the serving cup and mix well.
3. Pour boiling water into the serving cup with the mixture.
4. Cover the cup and steep it for 8 minutes.
5. You can mix in honey as per your taste.
6. Serve and enjoy it.

11. SOOTHING LEMON TISANE

Ingredients:

- 4 tbsp. lemongrass.
- 1 tbsp. lemon zest.
- 1 tbsp. lemon balm.
- 1 tsp. chamomile.
- ¼ tsp. stevia.

Instructions:

1. Boil the water in a pot.
2. Add all the ingredients to the serving cup and mix well.
3. Pour boiling water into a serving cup with lemon mixture.
4. Cover the cup and steep it for 8 minutes.
5. You can mix in honey as per your taste.
6. Serve and enjoy it.

12. MEADOW TEA

Ingredients:

- 5 tbsp. mint leaves.
- 1 tbsp. honey.

Instructions:

1. Boil the water in a pot.
2. Add mint and mix well.
3. Cover the pot and let it boil for 20 minutes at low flame.
4. Strain the tea in a serving cup.
5. Stir in honey.
6. Serve and enjoy it.

13. HERBAL INFUSION TEA

Ingredients:

- 1/2 tsp. rooibos tea.
- 1/2 tsp. ginger.
- 1/3 tsp. cloves.
- 1/2 tsp. cinnamon.
- 1/3 tsp. cardamom.

Instructions:

1. Add water to a pot and mix in all the ingredients.
2. Bring the water to boil for 20 minutes while covering the pot.
3. Strain the tea in a serving cup.
4. Serve and enjoy it.

14. LEMON AND ELDERFLOWER TEA

21

Ingredients:

- 1 tsp. honey.

- 1 tbsp. elderflower.

- 1 tsp. lime juice.

Instructions:

1. Boil the water in a pot.
2. Add all the ingredients and mix well.
3. Cover the pot and let it boil for 15 minutes at low flame.
4. Strain the tea in a serving cup.
5. Serve and enjoy it.

15. CHAMOMILE AND LEMON BALM

Ingredients:

- 1/3 tbsp. chamomile, dried.

- 1/3 tbsp. crushed dried leaves of lemon balm.

Instructions:

1. Boil the water in a pot.
2. Add all the ingredients and mix well.
3. Cover the pot and let it boil for 15 minutes at low flame.
4. Strain the tea in a serving cup.
5. Serve and enjoy it.

16. MINT TEA

Ingredients:

- 2 tbsp. rosemary.
- 3 tbsp. mint.

Instructions:

1. Add water to the pot and bring it to a boil.
2. Add rosemary and cover the pot for few minutes.
3. Add mint leaves to the cup and pour boiling rosemary water over it.
4. Cover the cup and let it steep for few minutes.
5. You can add lemon juice to enhance the taste.
6. Serve and enjoy it.

17. TULSI TEA

24

Ingredients:

- ¾ tsp. honey.

- 2 tbsp. Tulsi leaves (holy basil).

- 1 ½ tsp. lemon juice (optional).

Instructions:

1. Add water to the pot and bring it to a boil.
2. Add Tulsi leaves and let them boil.
3. Reduce the flame to low and cover the pot for 12 minutes.
4. Transfer the water into the serving cup.
5. Stir in lemon juice and honey and mix well.
6. Serve and enjoy it.

18. ASHWAGANDHA TEA

<u>Ingredients:</u>

- 1 ½ tsp. honey.
- 4 tbsp. Ashwagandha, dried.

<u>Instructions:</u>

1. Add water to a pot and mix in Ashwagandha.
2. Let it boil for 20 minutes.
3. Transfer the water into the serving cup.
4. Stir in honey and mix well.
5. Serve and enjoy it.

19. LEMON AND PEPPER TEA

Ingredients:

- ¾ tsp. turmeric.
- 1 tsp. honey.
- A pinch of pepper.

Instructions:

1. Add water to a pot and bring it to a boil.
2. Combine turmeric and pepper in a serving cup.
3. Transfer the boiling water to a serving cup with a turmeric mixture.
4. Mix it well.
5. Serve and enjoy it.

DECOCTIONS

A decoction is a concentrated liquid obtained from boiling or heating a material. The word decoction is commonly used for medicinal extract attained due to the herbal plant's heating bark, stem or roots. A decoction is different from an infusion in terms of the part of the plant used to obtain them, i.e., to gain infusion, the leaves or flower of the plant is used while collecting decoction bark, or root of the plant is used.

1. AMERICAN LIVER CLEANSING TONIC

Ingredients:

- 1/3 tsp. sassafras.

- 1/3 tsp. ginger.

- 1/3 tsp. dandelion

Instructions:

1. Add water to a pot and stir in the ingredients.
2. Bring it to a boil.
3. Reduce the flame to low and cover the pot.
4. Let it cook for 20 minutes.
5. Remove the pot from flame and keep it aside for 5 minutes while the lid is over the pot.
6. You may stir in honey if needed.
7. Serve and enjoy it.

2. BRONCHITIS SOOTHER

Ingredients:

- 1/3 tsp. colt foot.

- 1/3 tsp. marshmallow.

- 1/3 tsp. comfrey.

- 1/3 tsp. mullein.

Instructions:

1. Add water to a pot and mix in all the ingredients. Keep it aside for 20 minutes.
2. Place the pot over medium flame and let it boil.
3. Cover the pot and reduce the flame to low.
4. Let it cook for 20 minutes.
5. You may add honey as per your taste.
6. Serve and enjoy it.

This tea is best to get relief from asthma, sore throat, cough, bronchitis, and most respiratory system issues.

3. CHAGA MUSHROOM COFFEE

Ingredients:

- 2 tbsp. Chaga.
- 1 1/3 c water.

Instructions:

1. Add Chaga in water in a pot.
2. Place the pot over medium flame and let it boil.
3. Cover the pot and let it simmer for 15 minutes.
4. You may mix in honey as per your taste.
5. Serve and enjoy it.

This coffee acts as a stimulator for your immune system and prevents cancer development.

4. ECHINACEA DECOCTION

Ingredients:

- 1 tbsp. Echinacea.
- 1 ½ c water.

Instructions:

1. Add water to a pot and mix Echinacea root in it.
2. Place the pot over medium flame and bring it to boil.
3. Cover the pot and let it simmer for 35 minutes over low flame.
4. Transfer the decoction to the serving cup using the filter to remove the herb.
5. Serve and enjoy it.

This decoction will boost your immune system and will help you to fight various diseases.

5. HAWTHORN BERRY SYRUP

Ingredients:

- 1 ½ c water.

- 1 tbsp. of crushed hawthorn berry.

Instructions:

1. Combine hawthorn and water in a pot.
2. Place the pot over medium flame and let it boil.
3. Cover the pot and reduce the flame.
4. Let it simmer for 20 minutes.
5. Strain the syrup and preserve it for later use.
6. Use 1 tbsp. hawthorn syrup with honey in warm water and drink it once a day.
7. This decoction is best for cardiovascular diseases.

POPSICLES

1. FRUIT POPSICLES WITH COCONUT

34

Ingredients:

- 3 c coconut water.

- 5 slices of kiwi.

- ½ c black grapes.

- ½ c sliced strawberry.

- ½ c pineapple.

Instructions:

1. Combine all the fruits in a container.
2. Transfer the fruit mixture to the mold.
3. Fill the mold with coconut water.
4. Cover the mold and put it in the freezer for few hours.
5. Serve and enjoy it.

2. WATERMELON MINT POPSICLES

35

Ingredients:

- 5 c sliced watermelon.
- 1/3 c chopped mint.
- ½ c lime juice.

Instructions:

1. Add all the ingredients to the food processor and blend to get a smooth puree.
2. Strain the puree in a bowl.
3. Transfer the puree into the mold and put it in the freezer for a few hours.
4. Serve and enjoy it.

3. CUCUMBER MINT POPSICLES

<u>**Ingredients:**</u>

- 1/3 c lime juice.

- ½ c chopped mint leaves.

- 2 c Chopped cucumber.

- 2 c Water.

- 1/3 c Sugar.

- 1 tsp. green tea powder.

<u>**Instructions:**</u>

1. Add water to the pot and let it boil.
2. Stir in the sugar and reduce the flame to low.
3. Let the sugar dissolve to get syrup.
4. Mix in mint and stir well. Cook for few minutes to give syrup the flavor of mint.
5. Remove the pot from the flame and set it aside.
6. Remove the mint leaves from the syrup.
7. Place the mint syrup in the fridge for few minutes.
8. Add all the remaining ingredients to the blender and blend them to get a smooth puree.
9. Slowly add the mint syrup to adjust the taste.

10. Transfer the puree in mold and place it in the freezer
    for a few hours.

11. Serve and enjoy it.

4. MINT LEMON POPSICLES

Ingredients:

- 1 tbsp. lime peel.
- 2 tbsp. lemon juice.
- 3 c water.
- 3 tsp. honey.
- 1 c mint leaves.

Instructions:

1. Add water to a pot and bring it to a boil.
2. Mix in all the remaining ingredients and cook for few minutes to fully mix them.
3. Remove the pot from the flame and let it stand for a while.
4. Transfer the mixture to the mold and place in the freezer for few hours.
5. Serve and enjoy it.

5. PINE POPSICLES

Ingredients:

- ½ c pine needles.

- 3 c water.

- 3 lemon slices.

- 1 crushed clove.

- 1 tbsp. ginger.

- 1 tsp. green tea.

- 2 tbsp. lemon juice.

- ½ c jaggery.

Instructions:

1. Add water to the pot and bring it to a boil.
2. Mix in pine needles, clove and ginger. Cook for few minutes.
3. Now stir in the jaggery and let it boil for 5 minutes.
4. Mix in green tea and stir well.
5. Reduce the flame to low and cover the pot. Let it steep for 5 minutes.
6. Add lemon slices and remove the pot from the flame and let it stand for a while.
7. Strain the mixture in cups and set aside.

8. Place the cups in the freezer and freeze them for 80 minutes.

9. Serve and enjoy it.

6. STRAWBERRY BASIL POPSICLES

41

Ingredients:

- 1 c sliced strawberries.

- 1 tbsp. lemon zest.

- ½ c. sugar syrup.

- 1 ½ c basil leaves.

- ¼ c Tofutti cream.

Instructions:

1. Add lemon zest, ½ c basil leaves, strawberries and syrup in the food processor and blend to get a puree.

2. Transfer the strawberry puree into the mold and place it in the freezer for two hours.

3. Add cream, remaining basil and syrup in the blender and blend to get a smooth puree.

4. Remove the strawberry mold from the freezer and pour bail puree over it.

5. Place the mold again in the freezer and freeze for few hours.

6. Serve and enjoy it.

7. LAVENDER MOON MILK POPSICLES

Ingredients:

- 1 c coconut cream.
- ½ tsp. Ashwagandha powder.
- 2 tbsp. lavender.
- 1 ½ tbsp. honey.
- 1 vanilla bean.

Instructions:

1. Add cream in a bowl and whisk to get fluffy.
2. Add water and beat again to get 2 c
3. Place the bowl over medium flame.
4. Add vanilla beans and lavender and mix well. Cook for 5 minutes.
5. Remove the pot from the flame and set it aside.
6. Strain the mixture.
7. Add honey and Ashwagandha and toss well.
8. Place in fridge for 30 minutes.
9. Transfer the mixture into the mold and place it in the freezer.
10. Freeze for few hours. Serve and enjoy it.

8. LEMON VERBENA SUN TEA POPSICLES

43

Ingredients:

- 2 c Water.
- 1 c pineapple juice.
- 2 tbsp. verbena.

Instructions:

1. Add verbena and water in a jar. Cover the jar and shake well.
2. Place the jar in the sunshine for few hours to extract the essence of the herb.
3. Strain the mixture and set it aside.
4. Add pineapple juice to the mixture and toss well.
5. Transfer the mixture to the mold and place the mold in the freezer and freeze for few hours.
6. Serve and enjoy it.

ICE CUBES

1. BASIL AND ALOE VERA ICE CUBES

45

Ingredients:

- 1 c. basil.

- 2 tbsp. Aloe Vera gel mixture.

Instructions:

1. Add basil leaves in the blender with water and blend to get a smooth mixture.
2. Add Aloe Vera gel and toss well.
3. Transfer the mixture to an ice cube tray and place it in the freezer.
4. Freeze for few hours.

2. MINT ICE CUBES

Ingredients:

- Mint leaves
- Water

Instructions:

1. Add mint leaves to the ice cube tray and pour in water to fill the tray part.
2. Place the tray in the freezer and freeze.

3. GINGER AND GARLIC ICE CUBES

Ingredients:

- 1 c garlic.
- 1 c ginger.

Instructions:

1. Add garlic and ginger to a food processor and blend to get a paste.
2. Transfer the paste to the ice cube tray and place it in the freezer.
3. Freeze for few hours.

4. LIME ICE CUBES

Ingredients:

- Lemon juice

Instructions:

1. Add the lemon juice to the ice cube tray and freeze it for several hours.

5. COFFEE ICE CUBES

Ingredients:

- 4 tbsp. coffee.
- 2 c. Water.

Instructions:

1. Add water to the pot and bring it to a boil.
2. Mix in coffee and stir well.
3. Cook for few minutes.
4. Remove the pot from the flame and let it stand for few hours.
5. Transfer the coffee solution to an ice cube tray and freeze for few hours.

6. MASALA TEA ICE CUBES

Ingredients:

- 1 ½ c. Water.
- 1 star anise.
- 1 cardamom stick.
- 3 cloves.
- 2 tbsp. ginger.
- 1 tbsp. black pepper.
- ½ c. milk.
- 4 tbsp. black tea leaves.
- 1 tbsp. sugar.

Instructions:

1. Add water to the pan and bring it to a boil.
2. Mix in all the spices and cook for 15 minutes.
3. Stir in milk and reduce the flame to low.
4. Cover the pan and simmer it for 5 minutes.
5. Add black tea leaves and mix well. Cook for another 5 minutes.
6. Strain the tea and let it stand for few minutes. Transfer the tea into the ice cubes tray and freeze.

7. CUCUMBER AND LEMON ICE CUBES

Ingredients:

- 1 c. cucumber.

- 4 tbsp. of lemon juice.

Instructions:

1. Add cucumber and lemon juice in a blender and blend to get a puree.
2. Transfer the puree into an ice cube tray and freeze it for several hours.

8. BERRY CUBES

Ingredients:

- Berries (strawberry, blackberry and blueberry.)
- Water.

Instructions:

1. Add berries to the ice cube tray and pour it with water.
2. Place the tray in the freezer and freeze for few hours.

9. HOT CHOCOLATE ICE CUBES

50

Ingredients:

- 3 tbsp. cocoa powder.
- 1 tsp. vanilla essence.
- 2 c. Milk.

Instructions:

1. Add milk to a pan and boil it.
2. Add cocoa powder and vanilla and stir well.
3. Cook for few minutes to completely dissolve everything well.
4. Transfer the mixture to the ice cube tray and freeze.

<u>BATHS</u>

1. RELAXING HERBAL FOOT BATH

Ingredients:

- ½ c. lavender.
- 1 c. sage.
- ½ c hops.
- ¼ c. rosemary.

Instructions:

1. Add water to the pan and let it boil.
2. Add the herbs and stir well.
3. Cover the pan and reduce the flame.
4. Let it simmer for 15 minutes.
5. Transfer the mixture basin and add water.
6. Cover the basin with a sheet to contain the loss of heat.
7. Dip your feet and relax for 25 minutes.

2. HERBAL FACE STEAM

Ingredients:

- 1 tbsp. thyme.

- 1 tbsp. lavender.

- 1 tbsp. basil.

- 1 tbsp. eucalyptus.

- 1 tbsp. rosemary.

- 1 tbsp. peppermint.

- 1 tbsp. oregano.

Instructions:

1. Boil water in the pot over medium flame.
2. Add herbs in a wide mouth pot and pour in boiling water.
3. Mix well and cover the pot with the lid and leave for 3 minutes.
4. Before leaning over the pot to get steam, check the temperature not to burn your skin.
5. Lean over the pot and slowly inhale and exhale for about 10 minutes.

3. HERBAL BATH SALTS

<u>**Ingredients:**</u>

- 3 c. salt, Epsom and Himalayan pink.

- ½ c. Baking soda.

- 3 tbsp. olive oil.

- ½ c. rose petals, dried.

- 6 tsp. lavender oil.

- 6 tsp. rosemary oil.

- ½ c lavender flower, dried.

- 8 tsp. cardamom oil.

- ½ c basil, dried.

<u>**Instructions:**</u>

1. Combine all the ingredients in a food processor and blend to get a paste.

2. Transfer the paste into the jar and store it for later use.

3. Add 4 tbsp. of the paste into the bathing water and stir well.

4. Enjoy your relaxing and medicating bath.

4. ANTI-INFLAMMATORY BATH TEA

55

Ingredients:

- ½ c. ginger.

- 5 c water.

- ½ c birch bark, dried.

- 2 c Epsom salt.

- ½ c. yarrow, dried.

Instructions:

1. Add water in a pot over medium flame.

2. Add bark and ginger and stir well.

3. Let it boil and reduce the flame to low, and cover the pot.

4. Cook for 15 minutes.

5. Mix in yarrow and cook for another 10 minutes.

6. Strain the mixture, and anti-inflammatory bath tea is ready.

7. Add the mixture into the bathing tub and enjoy your bath.

COMPRESSES

Compresses are the wet and heavy towel or washcloth that is soaked in a cold or hot herbal decoction or infusion, which can be applied on any body part to relax it and compresses help to enhance the body healing process.

1. COLD HERBAL COMPRESSES

Ingredients:

- 1 green tea bag.

- 1 peppermint tea bag.

- 1 chamomile lavender tea bag.

- 1 c water.

- Eucalyptus essential oil

- Lavender essential oil

Instructions:

1. Add water to a pot and let it boil.

2. Add tea bags in a cup.

3. Pour in boiling water and cover the cup.

4. Let it steep for 25 minutes.

5. Soak a towel or washcloth in tea solution and let it there for a few minutes.

6. Gently squeeze to remove extra liquid.

7. The washcloth should be wet, but no liquid dripping is there.

8. Now drizzle 1 tbsp. Eucalyptus essential oil over the wet washcloth.

9. Apply this medicated washcloth around your feet, chest, anywhere you want.

This herbal compresses remedy will help you relax during summer, give smoothness to your eyes and may also enhance the glow of your skin.

2. HOT HERBAL POUCH

Ingredients:

- 2 tbsp. ginger.

- 10 Eucalyptus leaves.

- 5 tbsp. lime peel.

- 2 tbsp. lemongrass.

- 1 tbsp. tamarind powder.

- 2 tsp. salt.

- 3 tsp. camphor granules.

Instructions:

1. Combine all the ingredients in a bowl.
2. Transfer the mixture to a washcloth and make a pouch and tie it.
3. Place the pouch in hot water and massage the targeted area.

3. LAOTIAN HERBAL COMPRESS

Ingredients:

- 8 tbsp. cooked rice.
- 2 tbsp. basil.
- 3 tbsp. lemongrass.
- 3 tbsp. peppermint.
- 2 tbsp. ginger.
- 4 tbsp. cinnamon.

Instructions:

1. Combine all the ingredients in a bowl.
2. Transfer the mixture to a washcloth and make a pouch and tie it.
3. Place the pouch in hot water and massage the targeted area.

4. CHAMOMILE COLD COMPRESS FOR FEVER

Ingredients:

- 4 c hot water.
- 2 tsp. chamomile tea.
- Ice cubes.

Instructions:

1. Add water to a pan and mix in chamomile tea.
2. Cover the pan and let it steep for few minutes.
3. Let it stand for a while to cool it down.
4. Soak the washcloth in the tea mixture and squeeze the extra liquid.
5. Place the washcloth over the targeted area for more than 10 minutes and experience the effect.

5. BALI HERBAL COMPRESS BALL

Ingredients:

- 3 tbsp. ginger.

- 3 cloves.

- 5 tbsp. rice powder.

- 1 tbsp. turmeric powder.

- 1 tbsp. coriander.

- 1 tbsp. cinnamon.

Instructions:

1. Combine all the ingredients in a bowl and toss well to mix everything.

2. Transfer the mixture to a washcloth and fold to make a ball.

3. Tie the cloth with the yarn.

4. Add water to a pan and bring it to a boil.

5. Place the herbal compress in the boiling water for 30 minutes.

6. Remove the ball from water and let it stand for a while. When the temperature is bearable, use it on the targeted area.

POULTICES

1. HERBAL HEALING SALVE

Ingredients:

- ½ c calendula almond oil.
- 1/3 c beeswax.
- ½ c comfrey almond oil.
- ½ tsp. essential oil of rose geranium.
- ½ c plantain infused almond oil.
- 8 tbsp. herbal mixture.

Instructions:

1. Add herb mixture in the jar and pour over the almond oil.
2. Close the lid and shake well.
3. Place the jar in a warm place for more than 65 days.
4. Strain the oil from the mixture using cheesecloth and discard the solids content of the mixture.
5. Store at the dim place. The infused oil for the salve is ready.
6. Now add water to a pot and let it boil.
7. Add beeswax to the small pan and place the pan over boiling water to melt the wax.

8. When the wax is melted, add infused oils in it and stir well.

9. Remove the pan from the boiling water and set it aside for a while.

10. It will take few hours to cool down.

11. The healing salve is ready to use.

2. HERBAL POULTICE

Ingredients:

- 1 tsp. turmeric powder.

- 2 tsp. coconut oil.

- ¼ c sliced onion.

- 1 tsp. garlic.

- 4 tbsp. ginger paste.

Instructions:

1. Combine all the ingredients in a pan and cook over low flame until the content gets dry.

2. Remove the pan from the flame and let it stand for a while.

3. Transfer the mixture into the cheesecloth and fold the cloth and tie it.

4. Message the affected area with the pouch for about 30 minutes.

5. This poultice is used as an anti-inflammatory agent.

3. BRAN POULTICE

Ingredients:

- Water.

- Bran.

Instructions:

1. Add water to a pot and boil it.

2. Add bran and mix well to form a paste.

3. Apply while hot on the affected area.

4. This poultice can be used to get relieve strains, bruises and inflammation.

4. MUSTARD POULTICE

Ingredients:

- Mustard powder.
- Water.
- Flour.

Instructions:

5. Add mustard powder in water and make a paste.
6. Use flour to thicken the paste.
7. Add in a cloth and message.
8. It can be used to treat arthritis and to improve circulation.

5. BREAD POULTICE

<u>**Ingredients:**</u>

- Bread.

- Milk.

<u>**Instructions:**</u>

1. Add milk to a pot and heat it over medium flame.

2. Keep it aside to cool down a little.

3. Add bread slices and let them stand in the warm milk.

4. Mix bread with the milk to form a paste.

5. Now, apply over the skin and leave it for about 20 minutes.

6. You can use it on a cyst, splinter and abscess.

6. POTATO POULTICES

Ingredients:

- Shredded potato.
- Water.

Instructions:

1. Add water to a pan and boil it.
2. Add grated potato and make a paste.
3. Apply over the inflamed area for 10 minutes.
4. It can be used as a pain reliever and provides a cooling effect. Apply on carbuncles and boils.

CHAPTER 2:
MEDICINAL PLANTS OF NATIVE AMERICANS AND RECIPES

2.1. MEDICINAL PLANTS USED DAILY BY NATIVE AMERICANS

Butterbur.	Rosemary.
Goldenseal.	Reishi.
Mullein.	Tea Tree.
Oat seed.	Thyme.
Green tea.	Turmeric.
Devils club.	Food (as natural medicine).
Alpha-lipoic acid.	Garlic.
Alfalfa.	Comfrey.
Arnica.	Lemon balm.
Black haw.	Ashwagandha.
Black cohosh.	Parsley.
Boneset.	Dill.
Cinnamon.	Fennel.
Elder.	Catnip.
Eucalyptus.	Chives.
Evening primrose.	Bay leaves.
Milk thistle.	Winter savory.
Mint.	Stevia.
Motherwort.	Lemongrass.
Bettles.	Bergamot.

Plantain.	Oregano.
Burdock.	Sage.
Dandelion.	California poppy.
Willow.	Ginger.
Black Walnut.	Aloe Vera.
Jewelweed.	Calendula.
Red clover.	Marshmallow Root.
Yarrow	Astragalus herbs.
Anise.	Licorice root.
Chervil.	

2.2. SACRED RECIPES

1. CHICKEN KNEW

Ingredients:

- 2 chicken breast pieces.
- ½ c Butter.
- 2 eggs.
- 1 tbsp. garlic paste.
- 2 tbsp. parsley.
- Flour as required.
- Breadcrumbs as required.

Instructions:

1. Add garlic, parsley, salt and butter in a blender and blend to obtain a smooth paste.
2. Transfer the mixture in cling film and place it in the freezer for more than half an hour.
3. Make a pocket inside the chicken breast pieces.
4. Fill the chicken pocket with the garlic paste and close the mouth.
5. Dip the chicken piece in egg and roll it in flour and breadcrumbs.
6. Place the coated chicken pieces on a plate and place them in the fridge for few minutes to stand it.

7. Heat oil in saucepan and fry chicken pieces over medium flame for 5 minutes from both sides.

8. Transfer the pieces to the baking tray and bake in preheated oven at 250 F° for 15 minutes.

9. Serve and enjoy it.

2. SCARED PAN PEPPERS

Ingredients:

- Oil as required.
- 1 c chopped onions.
- Seasonings as required.
- 1 c chopped bell pepper.

Instructions:

1. Heat oil in a saucepan over medium flame.
2. Add onions and fry them for 5 minutes.
3. Add chopped bell peppers and seasonings.
4. Stir well and cook for 10 more minutes with frequent stirring.
5. Serve and enjoy it.

3. NATIVE AMERICAN ACORN SOUP

<u>**Ingredients:**</u>

- 3 c acorn.

- 1 c chopped carrot.

- 2 chopped celery.

- 1 chopped onion.

- 4 tbsp. butter.

- 1 ½ c mushroom.

- ¼ c vinegar.

- 4 c chicken broth.

- ½ tsp. cayenne.

- Salt to taste.

- ½ c yogurt.

- ½ c toasted pine nuts.

<u>**Instructions:**</u>

1. Add hot water to a bowl and add mushrooms to it. Keep it aside for half an hour.

2. Melt butter in the pan and add carrot, onion and celery and sauté for 5 minutes.

3. Stir in acorn bits and mushrooms. Cook for 6 more minutes.

4. Sprinkle salt and toss well.

5. Transfer the mixture to the blender and blend to obtain the puree.

6. Shift the puree in the pan again and stir in yogurt. Toss well.

7. Serve and enjoy it.

4. CORN COB JELLY

Ingredients:

- 2 c corn.

- 4 c sugar.

- 2 c fruit pectin.

- 5 c water.

- 1 tsp. food color.

Instructions:

1. Add corn cobs in boiling water and cook until fully boiled.
2. Take out the cobs and collect the liquid.
3. Add liquid to a pan and mix in sugar.
4. Stir to dissolve the sugar and let it cook for 10 minutes.
5. Add pectin and stir for 1 minute.
6. Remove the pan from the flame and set it aside.
7. Store in clean airtight jars.

CHAPTER 3: TRADITIONAL RECIPES OF NATIVE AMERICANS

3.1. TRADITIONAL LAKOTA

The Lakota literal meaning is "allies" or "friends," which is among the original tribe of native America. They lived in the Rocky Mountains before the Europeans came to invade this place.

According to them, food is a sacred entity that should be treated sacred and given due respect because there is no life on Earth without food. So they have devised unique methods to grow and maintain the food. The main source of food for them is bison, a rich source of protein and fat. Besides the bison, they also eat vegetables, fish, fruits and turkey. They gather the vegetables and fruits from different places and don't grow them because they are nomadic people, thus gathering them or trading them with local people. The vegetables they mostly eat are tipsily (cooked and make bread from it), blow, pain, wagmiza (to make soup). While the fruits that they commonly use are can, gooseberries, Saskatoon berries, strawberries, raspberries.

Some of the traditional foods used by Lakota, and in this book most commonly, and widely used recipes are shared.

1. WHOOPI SOUP

83

Ingredients:

- 4 c bison meat, cooked.

- 5 c beef stock.

- 3 sliced carrots.

- Salt to taste.

- 3 diced potatoes.

- Black pepper to taste.

Instructions:

1. Add broth to the pot and add all the ingredients to it.
2. Cover the pot and let it simmer for 50 minutes.

2. WASNA

Wasna is the traditional way of preserving meat for years.

Ingredients:

- Meat.

- Chokecherry (optional).

Instructions:

1. Braise the meat first.
2. Then, using a stone beat to pulp the meat.
3. Mix some of the dried chokeberries with the meat to make different variations of the Wasna, or mix it with fat and transfer the mixture in an airtight bag.
4. Seal the bag, and meat is preserved for almost four years.

3. WOJAPI

85

Wojapi is a berry soup liked by Lakota.

Ingredients:

- 3 c. berries (frozen).
- 1 ½ c sugar.
- 5 tbsp. cornstarch.
- 9 c water.

Instructions:

1. Add water in a pot and add berries. Let it simmer for 65 minutes.
2. Use an immersion blender to mash the content of the pot.
3. Slowly add the cornstarch mixture with constant stirring.

3.2. AMERICAN INDIAN FOOD LIST

Vegetables

- Beans.

- Cassava.

- Pumpkin.

- Tomatoes.

- Bell Pepper.

- Potatoes.

- Jerusalem artichoke.

Fruits

- Avocado.

- Blueberry.

- Cranberry.

- Squash.

- Pineapple.

- Guava.

- Corn.

- Acorn.

- Papaya.

- Quinoa.

- Strawberry.

- Amaranth.

- Grains.

- Cocoa.

- Wild rice.

Nuts and Seeds

- Black walnut.

- Peanut.

- Sunflower

- Cashew.

- Pecan.

Meat

- Turkey.

- Bison.

Sugar and spices

- Vanilla.

- Allspice.

- Maple.

3.3. NATIVE AMERICANS DIET

Native American's diet is focused on local food. They believe that eating the food grown in soil that the creator has given them will not honor the creator, and they try to avoid synthetic and processed food. They also believe that the creator has provided everything at walking distance from the area. These foods grown in the soil around us have every nutrient that our body needs. These are the staple food of our area; we should grow, eat and enjoy them. They use to eat according to the land they are in and the climate of that particular area.

Cold Weather

The cold weather increases the need for heavy food like meat (its fat), squash, potatoes and wild rice (their starches) and food that can be preserved for winter. Thus may also include the dried natural products such as dried berries, corn pemmican, etc.

Summertime

In summer, people have more energy and are active thus need high-energy food such as nettles, fish and berries. The soil provides green vegetables in the summer season, thus a rich source of fiber, proteins and starch. In summer amount of meat in the diet is reduced because they don't hunt much due to the high temperature in which they cannot preserve meat for a longer period.

Springtime

As we all know, springtime is to renew yourself, and the same is the case with the food. They eat eggs, fresh shoots like sprouts, dandelion, Purslane mint, ferns, and many others because these foods assist the body to detoxify itself, thus repairing and reorganizing the body.

Autumn time

In this season, they mostly harvest what they have sown and getting ready for winter. Tubers like yams, potatoes, carrots, apples, nuts, squash and vegetables are collected, used and stored for winters.

Below is the diet pyramid of Native Americans.

A Guide to
Daily Food
Choices
KEY
These symbols show fats, oils,
and added sugars in foods.
Fat
(Naturally occuring
and added)
Sugars
(added)
Fat's, Oils & Sweets
use sparingly
Low or Non-fat Dairy Products
Milk, Yogurt & Cheese Group
2-3 Servings
Meat, Poultry, Fish, Dry Beans
Eggs & Nuts Group
2-3 Servings
Vegetable Group
3-5 Servings
Fruit Group
2-4 Servings
WILD RICE
OATS
Bread, Cereal Group
6-11Servings
Rice, Pasta Group
6-11Servings

3.4 NATIVE AMERICAN CHRISTMAS RECIPES

1. QUINOA AND WILD RICE STUFFED SQUASH

Ingredients:

- 12 sweet squash.
- 1 tbsp. olive oil.
- ½ c pecans, chopped.
- 2 c. celery, chopped.
- 1 ½ c. wild rice.
- 1 ½ c. quinoa.
- 1/3 c. cherries, chopped.
- 2 chopped onions.
- 5 c. vegetable stock.
- 2 tbsp. chopped Sage leaves.
- 2/3 c. chopped apricot.
- Salt to taste.
- 1/3 c. cranberries, chopped.

Instructions:

1. Place squash in a pan and pour in water.
2. Bake in preheated oven at 300 F° for 40 minutes.
3. Sauté pecans in a pan over medium flame for 7 minutes. Transfer them to a plate.

4. Add onions, oil and celery to a pan and cook for 8 minutes over medium flame.

5. Pour in Sage, rice and broth and toss well.

6. Let it boil. Cover the pan and let it simmer for 30 minutes.

7. Add quinoa and toss.

8. Again simmer while covering the pan for 25 minutes.

9. Mix in the remaining ingredients and pecan and toss well. The stuffing is ready.

10. Remove the seeds from the squash and fill it with the filling.

11. Serve and enjoy it.

2. SUNCHOKE DIP

94

Ingredients:

- 1 ½ lb. artichokes.

- Salt to taste.

- 2 garlic cloves

- Red corn chips as required.

- 3 tbsp. lemon juice.

- 1 ½ tbsp. jalapeno chilies.

- 3 tbsp. olive oil.

Instructions:

1. Add water to a pot and boil it.

2. Add artichokes and cook for 15 minutes over medium flame.

3. Add all the ingredients, including the artichokes, to a blender and blend to get a puree.

4. Serve and enjoy it.

3. CORNICE CREAM

<u>Ingredients:</u>

- 1 ¼ c corn, cooked.

- 1 tsp. vanilla.

- 1 ½ c Cream.

- 5 egg yolk

- ½ c. sugar.

- 1 ¼ c milk.

<u>Instructions:</u>

1. Add corn (1 c) and cream (1/4 c) in a food processor and blend to get a puree.
2. Transfer the puree to the pan and add the remaining cream and corm and cook over high flame.
3. Add beaten egg yolk and stir well. Cook for nine more minutes.
4. Add vanilla and toss well.
5. Shift the pan over cold water and keep on stirring the mixture to lower the temperature.
6. Cover the pan and place it in the fridge for few hours.
7. Transfer the mixture to the ice cream maker and blend it.
8. Serve and enjoy it.

3.5 MANLY MAN HERBAL TEA RECIPES

1. TEA FOR MEN'S HEALTH

Ingredients:

- 1 tsp. basil.
- ½ tsp. ginkgo leaves.
- 1 tsp. ginseng root.
- ½ tsp. molasses.
- 1 tsp. hawthorn berries.
- ½ tsp. ginger.
- ½ tsp. saw palmetto.

Instructions:

1. Combine ginger and molasses in a bowl and mix well.
2. Add the remaining ingredients and whisk them.
3. Transfer the mixture to the jar and store.
4. Use 1 tbsp. of the mixture in hot water and cover the cup for 8 minutes. Drink and enjoy it.

2. TEA BLEND FOR MEN

Ingredients:

- 3 c. goat weed.
- 3 stars anise.
- 2 tbsp. ginger.
- 2 tbsp. dandelion leaves.
- 3 tbsp. hawthorn.
- 2 tbsp. nettle leaves.
- 2 tbsp. cinnamon.
- 1 tbsp. sarsaparilla.
- ½ tbsp. clove.
- ½ tbsp. yam.
- ½ tbsp. cardamom.

Instructions:

1. Combine all the ingredients in a jar and store them in the dark.
2. Use one tbsp. of the mixture to make the tea and drink.

3.6. HOW TO MAKE A GINGER TINCTURE?

1. EASY TO MAKE HOMEMADE GINGER TINCTURE RECIPES

Ingredients:

- 500 g. ginger roots.
- Apple cider vinegar as required.
- Honey as required.

Instructions:

1. Add the grated ginger to a jar.
2. Fill and add all the ingredients except for honey in a pan.
3. Cover the pan and let it boil.
4. When it starts boiling, lower the flame and simmer it for 60 minutes.
5. Remove the pan from the flame and cool it.
6. Mash the mixture with the help of a spoon.
7. Strain the mixture into a container and discard the solid content.
8. Add honey into the strained liquid and mix to dissolve it.
9. Transfer the mixture to the airtight container.
10. Place the container in the fridge.
11. Use 3 to 4 tbsp. of the mixture to boost your immune system regularly, especially in winters.

3.7. HOW TO MAKE OLD FASHIONED TONIC SYRUPS FOR WINTER COLD AND FLU

1. GRAPEFRUIT SEED EXTRACT

One of the oldest tonic syrup used by Native Americans and worldwide is grapefruit seed extract. The extract of grapefruit is a rich source of antioxidants, boosting your immune system. Thus, its use in winter can help you to fight seasonal cold and flu.

Ingredients:

- 1 c. grapefruit seeds.
- 3 tbsp. vegetable glycerin.
- 1 tbsp. ascorbic acid.

Instructions:

1. Bring the grapefruit seeds into powdered form by grinding or blending them in the blender.
2. Add the seed powder to water and stir well to dissolve it.
3. Strain the mixture and let it dry at a low temperature.
4. Add vegetable glycerin in a pan at medium flame.
5. Now stir in the concentrated seed powder and mix well.
6. Add ascorbic acid or any acid that is food safe.
7. Tightly cover the pan and let it heat for few minutes.

8. Remove the pan from the flame and cool it down to room temperature.

9. Strain the mixture to remove the particles.

10. Place the mixture in sunlight for few hours and store the concentrated tonic syrup for use in an airtight container at room temperature.

11. Add 8 to 10 drops of tonic syrup in water, juice, or anything liquid you like the most and drink it daily.

2. GINGER LEMON HONEY TEA

Ingredients:

- 15 lemon slices.
- 10 slices of ginger.
- Honey as required.

Instructions:

1. Add the slices of ginger and lemon to the jar.
2. Pour the honey into the jar and fill it.
3. Place the jar in the refrigerator.
4. After few days, the mixture in the jar will slowly turn into a soft jelly-like mixture.
5. Add 3 tbsp. of jelly mixture in hot water and mix well.
6. Cover the mug and let it steep for five minutes.
7. The ginger lemon as a cure and precaution to cold and flu in winter is ready.
8. Serve and enjoy it.

3. CATNIP TEA

Ingredients:

- ½ c catnip leaves.
- 2 c. water.
- 1 tsp. honey.
- 3 slices of lemon.
- 1 tsp. mint leaves.
- 1 tsp. thyme.
- 1 tsp. rosemary.

Instructions:

1. Add water to a pot and let it boil.
2. Transfer the boiling water into the teapot.
3. Add all the herbs to the teapot and stir well.
4. Cover the teapot and let it steep for 15 minutes.
5. The tea is ready.
6. Serve and enjoy it.

4. ELDERBERRY SYRUP

Ingredients:

- 4 c. water.

- 1 c. elderberries, dried.

- 2 tbsp. grated ginger.

- 1 tsp. cinnamon.

- 1 tsp. cloves.

- 1 cup. Honey.

Instructions:

1. Add all the ingredients except for honey in a pan.
2. Cover the pan and let it boil.
3. When it starts boiling, lower the flame and simmer it for 60 minutes.
4. Remove the pan from the flame and cool it.
5. Mash the mixture with the help of a spoon.
6. Strain the mixture into a container and discard the solid content.
7. Add honey into the strained liquid and mix to dissolve it.
8. Transfer the mixture to the airtight container.
9. Place the container in the fridge.
10. Use 3 to 4 tbsp. of mixture to boost your immune system regularly, especially in winters.

5. TEA TREE SYRUP

Ingredients:

- 4 c water.

- Leaves of tea tree.

Instructions:

1. Add water to a pot and bring it to a boil.
2. Add leaves of tea tree in boiling water.
3. Cover the pot and let it simmer for more than half an hour.
4. Strain the mixture and discard the solid content.
5. Store the strained liquid in an airtight container.
6. Use 5 to 6 tbsp. of the liquid to make a drink.
7. Serve and enjoy it.

3.8. HOW TO MAKE ROSEMARY TEA FOR MEMORY AND CIRCULATION?

Rosemary is a traditional herb commonly used to assist the body with digestion, improve circulation and memory, and give freshness to the brain and decrease fatigue and lethargy.

1. ROSEMARY TEA

Ingredients:

- 1 c. water.

- ¼ tbsp. chopped rosemary leaves.

Instructions:

1. Add water and chopped rosemary leaves in the deep pot at medium flame.
2. Cover the pot and let it boil.
3. Remove the pot from the flame and keep the cover on and let it settle for more than half an hour.
4. Remove the herbs from tea and serve.

2. ROSEMARY SYRUP

Ingredients:

- 4 c. water.
- 2 c. honey.
- 15-inch stem of rosemary.

Instructions:

1. Add water to a deep pot at a high flame and let it boil.
2. Separate leaves from the stems and place them left in the container.
3. Add boiling water in a rosemary container.
4. Cover the container with the lid and set it aside for half an hour.
5. Remove the rosemary leaves from the liquid.
6. Place the liquid on medium flame and add honey to it.
7. Stir until honey is fully dissolved in the liquid.
8. Serve and enjoy it.
9. You can also store the airtight syrup container for 20 days in the fridge.

CHAPTER 4: HERBAL REMEDIES FOR CHILDREN

4.1. 0–2 MONTHS

1. GRIPE WATER

Ingredients:

- 2 1/3 c. water.
- 1 ½ slice ginger.
- 2 tsp. chamomile, dried.
- 1/2 tsp. cardamom, dried.
- 2 tsp. crushed fennel.
- ½ tsp. coconut sugar.
- ¼ tsp. cinnamon.
- ¼ tsp. clove.

Instructions:

1. Add water to a deep pot at a high flame and let it boil.
2. Add all the ingredients except for cinnamon, sugar and clove in a cloth and tie a note.
3. Place the tied cloth in boiling water and remove the pot from the flame.
4. Cover the pot and let it steep for one hour.
5. Take out the cloth from the water and stir in the remaining ingredients and mix well.
6. Transfer the solution into the glass jar and seal it.
7. Place the jar in the freezer and freeze it.
8. Shake well before use and use half a tsp. for your child.

2. HOMEMADE POWDER FOR THE SOFT SKIN OF NEWBORN

Ingredients:

- 2 tbsp. kaolin clay (natural absorbent, uses as the base for baby powder.)
- 2 tbsp. powder of arrowroot (natural adsorbent).
- 3 drops of essential oil, chamomile (safe to use with soothing and anti-inflammatory properties.)
- 3 drops of lavender oil.

Instructions:

1. Add kaolin clay and arrowroot in a bowl and mix well.
2. Now, mix in oils and combine the mixture well.
3. Shift the powder into a bottle.

3. YARROW RECIPE FOR BABIES

Ingredients:

- 1 tbsp. elderflower.

- 1 tbsp. yarrow.

- 1 tbsp. peppermint.

Instructions:

1. Mix flour, peppermint and yarrow in a bowl and toss well.

2. Shift the mixture to a storage container.

3. The yarrow balm is ready.

The balm can be used as an anti-inflammatory and anti-microbial agent in case of fever or injury.

4.2. 2–12 MONTHS

1. CREAMSICLE BATH

Ingredients:

- 3 tsp. essential oil of sweet orange.

- Lukewarm water.

- 2 tsp. vanilla oleoresin essential oil.

Instructions:

1. Add sweet orange essential oil for about three drops with two drops of vanilla oleoresin essential oil in lukewarm water and stir well.

2. Bath your child with this water and let him enjoy the freshness and sootiness that he will get after taking a bath.

<u>2. HERBAL BATH</u>

<u>Ingredients:</u>

- 1 tbsp. peppermint.
- 1 tbsp. lavender.
- 1 tbsp. chamomile.
- 1 tbsp. lemon balm.

<u>Instructions:</u>

1. Add the mixture of peppermint, lavender, chamomile and lemon balm into a cloth and tie a knot to keep the content inside.
2. Place the knotted cloth in warm water that you will use to give a bath to your baby. Stir well.
3. First, clean the burn area with cold water using a cotton cloth.
4. Then, add few drops of lavender in water and wash the burnt area with this lavender water.

Lavender gives a soothing effect on the burn area, acts as an antimicrobial, and enhances the skin repair system. This herbal bath is a good source of antiseptic and skincare for your baby. Herbal remedy for Burns

3. REMEDY FOR TEETHING

Ingredients:

- 5 tsp. chamomile.

- 3 tsp. vegetable oil.

Instructions:

1. Combine few drops of chamomile and vegetable oil in a small container.

2. Now, take 2 tsp. of the blend in a mini bowl and add cool water. Mix well.

3. Apply the mixture over the baby's gum using a cotton cloth.

4. Massage the area well. This will help to soothe the area and make the gum soft reduce the pain with teething.

4. BABY POWDER

Ingredients:

- 4 c cornstarch.

- 1 tbsp. kaolin clay.

- 1 tbsp. rose geranium essential oil.

- 4 c. arrowroot powder.

- 1 tbsp. sweet orange essential oil.

- ½ tbsp. ylang-ylang essential oil.

Instructions:

1. Combine corn starch, kaolin clay, and essential oil of rose geranium, arrowroot powder, essential oil of sweet orange and essential oil of ylang-ylang in a bottle.

2. Close the lid of the powder bottle and shake well to blend all the ingredients.

3. Apply on the skin of the baby but remember don't apply directly. First, transfer the powder into your hands and use your hands to apply the powder to the desired area.

4. This powder absorbs unnecessary moisture from the skin, and rose geranium will give a floral essence to the skin.

5. The powder will keep the skin of the baby smooth and
    silky.

4.3. 12 MONTHS–5 YEARS

1. ROSY ROLL-ON

123

Ingredients:

- 3 tsp. rosewood.

- 2 tsp. rosehip oil.

- 2 tsp. rose absolute.

Instructions:

1. Combine rosewoods, rosehip oil, and rose absolute in a container and mix well.

2. Transfer the mixture into the roll-on bottle and apply when required by the kid in summers.

2. LEG ROLLER

Ingredients:

- 3 tsp. cedar wood.

- 2 tsp. jojoba oil.

- 2 tsp. rosewood.

- 3 tsp. sweet marjoram.

Instructions:

1. To give relief to your kid in bed from itching or any restlessness, mix cedar wood, jojoba oil, rosewood and sweet marjoram. Shake them well and transfer them into the roll-on bottle.

2. Apply before bedtime and enjoy your sleep.

3. YOGA GROUND INHALER

125

Ingredients:

- 5 tsp. frankincense.
- 3 tsp. cypress.
- 3 tsp. rosewood.

Instructions:

1. Combine frankincense, cypress, and rosewood in an inhaler. Use it to enhance the immune system of your kid.

4. PALMAROSA CALMING AROMA

Ingredients:

- 6 tsp. coconut oil.
- 2 tsp. jojoba oil.
- 4 tsp. sandalwood.
- 4 tsp. Palmarosa oil.
- 1 tsp. patchouli.
- 1 tsp. rose geranium.
- 1 tsp. absolute oil.

Instructions:

1. Combine any body lotion (unscented) with coconut oil and jojoba oil along with sandalwood and Palmarosa oil each. Also, add patchouli, rose geranium and absolute oil.
2. Shake everything well to get a smoothly blended mixture.
3. Apply when need to soothe the body of your kid.

4.4. FIVE YEARS–12 YEARS

1. CARROT PUREE

Ingredients:

- 2 c. chopped carrots.
- ¾ c. water.
- ¼ tsp. nutmeg.

Instructions:

1. Boil water in a pot over a medium flame.
2. Add carrots and cover to cook it for 10 minutes.
3. Let it cool.
4. Add boiled carrots, half a cup of liquid and nutmeg in a food processor.
5. Add liquid to adjust the consistency of the mixture to the desired level.
6. Serve your child and enjoy it.

It is a source of beta-carotene, which protects the health of the eyes and an anti-oxidant source to keep your immunity strong and provides calcium to keep your bones strong.

2. APPLE NUTMEG

Ingredients:

- 2 c. Chopped apple.
- ¼ tsp. nutmeg.

Instructions:

1. Combine nutmeg and chopped apple in a container and steam it for 20 minutes to get a puree.
2. The apple-nutmeg puree is ready to use for your baby.

Apples are a rich source of vitamin C, anti-oxidants and fibers and strengthen your immune system. While nutmeg has inflammatory and anti-oxidant properties.

3. PEAR-NUTMEG PUREE

Ingredients:

- Water.

- 1 tsp. nutmeg.

- 2 c pear, chopped.

Instructions:

1. Add 1/3 c water, a pinch of nutmeg and 2 c chopped pear in a pan and mix well.

2. Cover the pan and let it cook for 20 minutes over medium flame with occasional stirring.

3. Remove the pan from the flame and let it cool down.

4. Blend the mixture in the food processor to obtain the smooth puree.

5. The combination of nutmeg and pear will help your baby in digestion and give relief to his tummy.

Listed below are some of the quick DIY remedies for young babies:

4. COLIC

Ingredients:

- 2 tsp. chamomile.

- 2 tbsp. lavender.

- 2 tbsp. almond oil.

Instructions:

1. Add two drops of chamomile and lavender in a bowl with 2 tbsp. almond oil. Mix them well.

2. Rub this oil as messaging oil over the tummy and back of the baby to give a soothing effect to make him relax.

5. EAR ACHES

Ingredients:

- 1 tsp. almond oil.

- 1 tsp. lavender oil.

Instructions:

1. Combine 1 tsp. almond oil and a drop of lavender oil.

2. Use cotton buds to clean the ears of the baby using the solution you just made.

3. Secondly, you can also use the mixture to massage the baby's ear from the backside of the ear to soothe him.

6. FEVERS

Ingredients:

- 6 tsp. chamomile.
- 5 tsp. lavender.
- Lukewarm water.

Instructions:

1. Combine lukewarm water with six drops of chamomile and lavender in a bowl.
2. Dip the baby wipe in the water mixture and wipe your baby to reduce the temperature.
3. Be patient and continue using the mixture to lower the temperature.

7. LEMON BATH

Ingredients:

- 3 tsp. grapefruit essential oil.

- 3 tsp. lemon juice.

Instructions:

1. Add 3 drops of essential oil of grapefruit and lemon in warm water and stir well.

2. Bath your baby from this water to keep his skin healthy.

8. BABY LOTION

Ingredients:

- 2 tbsp. coconut oil.
- 2 tbsp. coconut butter.
- 3 tsp. lavender essential oil.
- 2 tsp. chamomile essential oil.

Instructions:

1. Melt coconut oil and coconut butter in steam water and stir in 3 tsp. essential oil of lavender and chamomile oils. Mix to combine well.
2. Keep the mixture aside for a while to cool it down.
3. When cooled down, beat the mixture using a beater till the mixture is fully whipped.
4. Shift the mixture into the container. The baby lotion is ready.

CHAPTER 5:
BENEFITS OF HERBALISM

5.1. BENEFITS FOR NATIVE AMERICAN HERBALISM

Since ancient times herbalism has been an integral part of the medicinal world for curing diseases, including mild fever, cold, cough and flu to severe infections and allergies. Native Americans still believe in these traditional herbal tactics, but now most of the population is incorporating modern medicines in their conventional health treatment mechanisms. Thus, their healing beliefs and health practices are diverting their way. But is the fact that herbal treatment has always successfully secured a very distinctive place in the medicinal world with astonishing outcomes. For this reason, the importance of herbalism is inevitable.

Modern medicines are based on individualistic and mechanistic approaches, very helpful in fast recovery from mild to chronic illness. Still, it is a general trend that people are more inclined towards herbal treatment, and the popularity of these natural remedies is increasing with each passing day; because of the positive record of encouraging and healthy benefits of herbal products, the general public trusts more natural treatment than chemically synthesized allopathic formulas. Since the past few decades, a lot of work has been done on herbalism. Several research studies and clinical trials have proved the positive and healthy impact of herbal remedies. Many websites are referring to different manufacturers' available using Native American terms for their herbal remedies.

Herbal healing circles are now being integrated by the Native Americans into modern practices and are popular in community centers. The basic herbal treatment rules are the same; however, the discussion subjects have been changed to modern issues. A historian in California traveled to know about the NA-native American tribes and composed a considerable account. According to him, although most Native American tribes have moved to urban areas still, they believe in their traditional healing system. They consider natural herbal remedies the best alternative to modern health treatment systems. They are very much concerned about their cultural heritage of herbal treatments and identity. But with the changing demands of time, health-related issues are also varying. For example, diabetes and such chronic diseases were non-existent among the Native Americans around 1000 years ago but not such diseases are rapidly spreading.

This rapidly increasing diabetes incidence may be due to the modern way of work reservation, less physical activity, and consumption of highly processed food. Many research studies have shown that if Native American tribes return to their traditional herbal diet like fruits, wild games, and root vegetables, then the adverse effects of various metabolic disorders can be reversed. But there is a difficulty that different tribes have their own varying beliefs about such diseases. For example, people of the Navajo tribe believe that diabetes is caused by disharmony and other influences like white people. The people of northern Utes take diabetes as an entity taking possession of the people compelling them to do evil things. In short ancient native tribes in America believe illness to be brought upon deviance from the traditional ways.

However, it will be right to say that herbalism has been a staunch part of the medical world. Herbal medicines are composed of active ingredients. Many of these active agents are still unknown. Still, the herbal physicians believe that it will be more effective to these active agents than plants instead of using isolated versions of these active compounds. According to them, the effect of using the whole plant is greater than their parts. However, critical to these herbal treatments argue that sometimes it becomes difficult to prescribe the measured dose of any specific ingredient while using herbal medicines.

Herbal medicines play an important role in maintaining the natural balance of the human body. Different herbs react differently on body systems. Some herbs are found very commonly that may be prescribed to cure casual diseases like cough, cold or flu; however, there are some herbs available that require to be referred very consciously as their dose above the optimum quantity may cause adverse side effects it shows that herbalism is a separate medical branch. One should be an expert on herbalism before prescribing any medicine to the patient, as the concept of taking the herbal medicines completely safe is not right.

However, to emphasize the importance of herbal medicines, a few examples are quoted here. For example, the Echinacea herb stimulates the immune system, helpful in resisting various infections and treats the ailments like fever, herpes, and boils. The Dong Quai herbs are used to cure premenstrual tensions, period pain and symptoms of menopause. It also helps in lowering high blood pressure. Garlic an abundantly used plant to deal with high cholesterol levels, thus protecting from heart diseases and a very good antioxidant. It is also very beneficial to deal with several respiratory infections, colds, fever, and coughs. Ginger is useful for treating nausea and motion sickness. Ginkgo biloba herb helps in maintaining the circulatory system of the body and tinnitus. Ginseng herb is used to treat fatigue, high blood pressure, and high cholesterol. Hypericum herb is a very good antidepressant. This herb is used by various pharmaceutical companies in their anti-depression pills. It is also very useful to deal with insomnia and anxiety. But where herbal medicines have many benefits, some negative effects are also associated with their excessive use. One should not use any medicine without proper prescription and instruction by his/her physician. Always purchase the medicines from the pharmacist with a good market reputation and see the composition on the label wrap of herbal products. Be careful about the timings, dosage and consult your doctor if any irritating reaction is felt.

CONCLUSION

Native Americans find themselves very close to nature. They have built a connection with nature because they believe that it has the remedy to all the disease and for balance mind, body and soul in harmony with each other. With nature, only then a person and a society can stay healthier and happy. In this regard, they discovered many medicinal plants and have used them to prevent and treat several diseases. They have registered natural remedies from cold and flu to manly man recipes from remedies for one-day baby, to 60 years old man from bath recipes to foot massage. They wanted the world to make connections with nature and explore the hidden treasures in it for the benefit of mankind. The herbal remedies handed over from generation to generation are still very useful against many infections, working even better than the modern world cures because, modern medicines come at the cost of something the side effects, while herbal remedies are with benefits, no side effects.